Dead Reckoning

Dead Reckoning
Michael Jackson

Caroline Jane Bourne

December 2006 .

AUCKLAND UNIVERSITY PRESS

First published 2006

Auckland University Press
University of Auckland
Private Bag 92019
Auckland
New Zealand
www.auckland.ac.nz/aup

ISBN 1 86940 361 4
ISBN 978 1 86940 361 4

Publication is assisted by creative nz

Printed by Astra Print Ltd, Wellington

Contents

dead reckoning: calculation of one's position on the basis
of distance run on various headings since the last precisely
observed position, with as accurate allowance as possible
being made for wind, currents, compass errors, etc.

Webster's Dictionary of the English Language

Flying to Beirut

Let up the shade
only to be blinded by blueness
beyond the northern coast of Rhodes,
white hawsers of surf
haggard hills and die-cast villages,
the sea pitted like the surface of a gong.

Fragments of cloud are
spirited away
in a wind I cannot feel,
high above a ferry
ploughing west, the smear
of its wake, its slow Aegean
progress toward Ankara.

And so I come to my senses
after far too long
in another hemisphere,
imagining myself on one of these
white roads that may lead anywhere,
and the prospect tonight of Lebanon.

Walking to Pencarrow

It's the fourth of July.
I'm sitting on a rock
at Inconstant Head
with the sea seething and hissing
between gritted teeth
and the seaward Kaikouras
like mounded rock salt
in the south.

There are two white
lighthouses on the promontory
and I am thinking of friends
in Sierra Leone
as I walk toward them.
I also think of the rocks
under me and the rocks
on which the sea itself heaves –

all that anger out there
that has spelled such tragedy.
Today it has cast up
wrack and corroded
paua shells. I pick them up,
fitting one into another
like Chinese boxes
or Matryoshka Dolls

as if I might rebuild
the burned villages
and make whole
that which has been broken –
that world in which I once
staked everything
on knowing what I could not know,
and could not hold.

Ali

You are standing on the Freetown wharf
in police uniform as our ship prepares to leave,
your hands empty of the oranges
you brought on board for us . . .

But this was thirty years ago
before madness claimed you
before war engulfed your country
before your son was killed
before my daughter became a woman
before your brother phoned me this morning in Copenhagen
with the news that you were dead.

'Send me that photo you took of Ali on the wharf,'
he said. 'And come back soon.
We are rebuilding the house.
The road is now open to Firawa.
Everyone remembers you.'

My fingernails feel for the hard shallow rind
of African oranges. I squeeze the bittersweet juice
into my mouth,
and sit in my office after Sewa's call
in absolute silence.

Amputees' Camp, Freetown

Heaney with his Grauballe and
Tollund men might have focused on
the missing arm, its walnut burr and whorl
of skin from which I shrink, gone as far
as making their phantom pain
a metaphor for memory – the day
that they recall, slow-motion as in space,
a blunt machete sawing through a limb,
a screaming child, and all that followed
not in thought but flight.
                    We are voyeurs
whom bog-dark centuries keep safe.
Distant, these are not our kin.
He knows this best who has no words for it:
'They came at noon. By evening they were gone.
Twenty of us were dead, or bleeding
from our wounds. We were farmers.
What had we done to them?
We cannot forget, cannot forgive,
though life goes on.'
                    The halter at the neck
is nothing they can use. No fingerprints
identify the enemy, divine a cause.
Images of ridge and river, grain or tar
make damn all difference.

Here is no 'tribal, intimate revenge'.
Only the matter-of-fact phrases:
'Seed rice is all we ask. With seeds we can begin again.'

Vultures

These shabby, cursèd angels
were in the sky when I came here
in '69;
        now they descend
and show themselves
like common criminals,
        staggering and bickering
by the slaughtered bull,
and I find it almost impossible
to remember when they palmed the air,
        their wing tip feathers
fingering the invisible,
so high you could not see
their red necks craning,
        their scorched eyes combing
the earth for a kill.

Lumley Beach

Beached canoes
called *Keep the Faith* and *Stop the War,*
Sea Never Dry, Democracy,
and the buoyed arc
of a seine net hauled ashore,
a score of fishermen leaning on the rope,
two laying the slack net down . . .

And then a flabbergasted shoal
of karé poured onto the sky-
slicked sand
and beaten lifeless by the women
who have brought basins to harvest them.

But not enough to fill
the bellies here, and none to sell,
the silver, gasping catch
mocking their captors' hunger,
who wait as if at Galilee for a miracle.

I walk on over clouds
in the tide-line's patina,
past bars where UN workers drink
gin slings with local girls,
while out at sea an all but invisible
foreign trawler,
licensed to kill,
ploughs the near-empty ocean.

Troisième Âge

Sixty-five, and the thump of surf on ironsand
still drumming into my brain the lore I learned
on this black sea littoral as a child,
chalked by drift, erased by spume, spat on by rain.

Such was the rhetoric I used back then!
Oceanic in import, measured to beat the band.
But we are toughened by suffering
and words are shoals that shift, mere
pumice stone, bluffs that fall away.

So if I were in Mokau now, heading
toward Mount Messenger, I would not
shun anything that washed ashore – blue plastic
packing tape, odd shoes, unlabelled bottles
without ships or notes inside . . .

Though the sea in a conch complain:
'Who taught you how to sing? Who showed you
the ropes? Who gave you driftwood with which
to build? Who confided things no tongue
can tell? Who told you what to say?'

For What it's Worth

What if the world were subject to our will,
the seas obedient to our every wish
and the earth made fertile through our prayer?

What if not stepping on the sidewalk cracks
or folding linen obsessively
had the same effect as foreign aid,

and keeping the garden free from weeds, the lawn
well mown . . . all that care
translated into the general good?

Yet consider the burden we would bear
alone in our endless cleaning-up
as if a tidy house could make us more secure.

Or think of Adolf, his will-to-power,
his armies goose-stepping on the sidewalk cracks
the lives snuffed out by his signature.

Maybe it's just as well we don't clean up,
switch off the TV news when it gets too bad,
and place our trust in lotteries.

Setting the alarm, getting the shopping done,
letting the garden grow rank with weeds
beats putting an end to genocide.

And so I say, do your damnedest ocean, eat
your heart out earth! I'm going with the flow
for what it's worth.

Greta Point

The range like a hog-backed adze
this place I miss,
wind tearing the paper from my hand
as I scribble this.

Clouds welded together
sky and earth,
the annealed scar-tissue as cold as the sea,
and by the same sea buffeted.

But my soul's as steady
as a rock. Pohutukawa
pollen blown against the kerb,
as in the grass

a single cicada sings
of the lives I did not live,
raising my voice above the wind
shouting to be heard.

Customhouse Quay

She's out of sight
behind the black Brasilia,
Slav, I think, Ukrainian,
her soulful English,
dark eyebrows,
bewilderment.

We migrate or drift
to the antipodes
from God knows where,
clouds resembling barbed wire,
or a Balinese shadow
puppet play.

We are proverbial
ships in the night. If we met
we wouldn't know what to say;
age, appointments and circumstance
move us on. Though she, I guess,
will stay, taking orders,
wiping these surfaces,
working for a pittance
until the someone I used to be
comes her way.

Araucaria

My Jacob's ladder,
rung by rung
into the sky,
the dizzying depths
of it, this mast
to which I clung,
vertiginous suburbia
below me like the sea.

My childhood was Norfolk
Island all over again,
pining for where
clouds bore themselves away;
the siren shriek of blackbirds
was my ancestry,
the smell of privet
like stale sperm.

Cobalt for the empyrean,
silk cotton for cloud
but for the tufted green
of the araucaria
and its grey-green trunk
the only metaphor
is the ladder I drew up after me
as I disappeared.

No Circulars

All's square in love
and suburbia,
the parked cars
vacuumed and polished
the dry leaves
raked and burned.

I look around the
neighbourhood I left
for something more
than the sanctuary
of a wattle grove,
pine needles
in the sun,
a glimpse of the open sea,

wondering whether
the smell of laurels
crumbled in my hand
would sustain me here
if I returned.

Leaves

These I delighted in:
cocksfoot drawn
through my fingers
soft and vandalised,
clover busy with
bumblebees,
dandelion like
a child's sun,
plantain with which
to play at soldiers,
and buttercups
to see if one liked butter.

I imagine one now
under my chin
capturing
the yellowy vestige
of being young,
rub paspalum seeds
in the hollow of my hand
for the stickiness
that will hold things fast,
and breathe in
the smell of Tarata leaves
for what it brings to mind –
my *petite madeleine.*

Hi Santa!

The annual Santa Parade
has not been cancelled
because of unseasonal
weather or
because of your death.

None of the changes
that overwhelm us change
the route of the parade
or cloud the joy
of children
at the kerbside gathering
or spoil their gifts,
the picnic at the beach,
the released balloons.

This is where our singular
existences fall away
from what is shared
and the shared takes on
its singular destiny,
caring less for any one of us
than for the seemingly same
children always
on the tartan rugs,
their open sandals,
their paper flags
the Highland bands
and Santa waving!

Finisterre

The ends of the earth,
the westernmost
coast of Spain

or here at Reinga
where two seas contest
our separateness.

The night sky is
the depth of my longing,
the Milky Way
a fringing reef
around the coral island
I have become.

My e-mails evaporate
before I can save or send,
my bottled messages
bob back disconsolate
in the waves,
the phone is dead.

I'm marooned, my love!
With crosses, this prisoner
counts his days.
At Finisterre
his dawn's your dark,
his night your day.

Cenotaph

The stone soldier that stood over my childhood
still stands, his bowed lemon-squeezered head as if ashamed
of the white-washed uniform. His hands
muzzle a rusting .303.

On Anzac Day the base was wreathed with laurel. Red
poppies bloomed. *For the Fallen. Lest we Forget.* And after
the Town Hall service we tagged along as the town band played
marches to stir our blood.

My naïve eyes would pan from the pinstripe suits, the faded
silks of campaign medals, to the Maxim gun
cemented to the street. The nearby rhododendron
was, I knew, the biggest in the world.

Now they're gone – those that fell in Flanders mud
and at the Dardanelles, or survived to drink their 10,000 beers
in the Railway pub – the exhortations to remember
their 'sacrifice' fall on my deaf ears.

But the rhododendron's there, continuing to shade the Old
Man's Seat, as oblivious as the soldier to our brass
and poppies and promises. Only time decides
which sentiments were ours and which were theirs.

Byrne

My father's cousin Byrne
was a precision engineer, could turn
metal so exactly on his lathe
the shavings were like foil,
the finished thing fitting
so faithfully the box he made for it
it resembled the myrrh
the magus brought to Christ.

But no star lit the firmament
above Three Kings
where Byrne eked out his days;
blind behind his goggles
at the lathe, or squinting
through a lens, or red
from sleeplessness
when he emerged

from the shed in which he slaved.
I never figured what kept him there,
my 'Man in the Iron Mask', or what
he craved. He and his mum
would come for Xmas drinks,
white wine for her, ale for him,
his big hands grimed as he held
the glass and let me pour,
but gravely quiet all afternoon.

A man without a following;
always the same scuffed shoes
and shabby cardigan, yet cut
and turned such things as I have
never made, dying
intestate and alone, the stainless
steel, the valves, the perfect
gadgets unbequeathed.

Nothing symbolic, nothing
like the star, or column
on One Tree Hill. But still
I think of the empty glass he held
in his blunt hands, his shame,
his solitude, his singlemindedness,
as traits I have inherited –
his final testament and will.

Clifton Firth's Photographs

Auckland way back when.
I came upon the scene
without a history,
solely and unrepentantly myself,
death a conceit of poetry,
knowing no sudden loss
or slow decay,
as if I owned the present, no one else.

Here Clifton Firth memorialised
glamorous women with whom
few now identify,
and young Americans
from the Pacific war
who stare at the camera
as if on orders to.

Forgotten plates
from a forgotten studio
salvaged only hours before
the demolition crew
moved in:
Ron Mason, who Baxter claimed
as 'our own Camus';
Lowry for whom I worked
in that basement room on Airedale Street;
Glover who said he was 'indomitable',
and Fairburn, Rouault's clown,
whose 'Cave' disclosed for me
the suffering behind
those hessian landscapes of McCahon's.

19

When I left the City Library
rain had cleared the air,
Waiheke visible, and beyond
the pale blue outline of Great Barrier.
So spirits go
from scoria to ether,
paling into sky
the barest memory.

So we take up
these lives deferred,
bruising our own way through
the traffic and the built-up littoral,
until in time we too are little more
than pictures from
an exhibition
pinned to a spot-lit wall,
saved not from death
but a wrecking ball.

The Discovery of Mallory's Body

Why, I do not know,
but I imagine it is myself
they have found frozen
under the summit of Everest,

the braided and bleached
climbing rope still coiled
around the torso, skin
as white as marble,

upper body wedded to the ice,
and the broken leg
with its perfectly preserved
hobnailed boot.

Why do I see these as
the misidentified remains
of my own life
and crave to be lost

to consciousness again,
a letter from my wife against my heart,
the weather closing in,
and then the dark

in the utterly unconscious space
of Everest? And why do I peer
like a voyeur at the web page
called mountainzone

the news relayed
by satellite, the photo
and the name,
unless I want to retrieve my life

from where I left it
all those years ago
when my first wife's death
sent me snowblind

into a place of whiteouts
and thin air.
Now I come back
like Mallory

to a world I barely
recognise, lives
that have passed me by,
old friends for whom

I am as good as dead.
Better perhaps to lie
back broken in that
oblivion, one's body

ageless in an icefall
than return to where
one imagines it is possible
to make it to the top

without oxygen
leading one's own anonymous
life at the end of a rope
climbing nowhere.

Tsunami Theodicy

The nuns at my daughter's school
have been saying that the tsunami
was God's way of testing our faith;
'I don't believe in God; God's cruel,'
my daughter says. 'But I still like Jesus;
he'd never do anything like that.'

We misinterpret *Genesis*.
Earth was never a void, a nothingness
to which God brought light.
Creation was *always* going on,
without beginning, without end.
Forever incomplete.

God's like a bad teacher, I tell
my daughter, cruel to be kind.
He has much to learn. Sometimes
he gets it wrong, breathing too hard
over the waters, for instance,
forgetting to separate sea from dry land.

Body and Soul

Like two transparencies
the old face overlays the young;
and in its blotched complexion,
broken veins, we glimpse
the one whose life we thought
would never end, to whom we swore
undying love.

The old, asleep, seem dead.
Slack-jawed, their mouths agape,
they beg for burial,
but half-wake appears
the flame that used to burn –
the animus, the soul!

Kuranko say one's life
'goes out' at night
(only the body sleeps)
to forage, farm, or feast
or seek revenge. It has
its own agenda and itinerary;
one's body simply harbours it
and waits for its return.

So do the old confess
that they have never aged
(only their bodies have),
the vertebrae collapsed,
the organs giving in,
and so it is that they
conceive a world more just
in which the ceaseless longing soul's
contained in flesh more durable,
its life less onerous.

After Babel

What moved the men of Shinar
to build with brick and slime
their storied tower?

Was it a name
that kept them unified?

And why should God
destroy this unity
scattering them one by one
across the world?

I've never mastered
another tongue
always wondering
what was the language that we lost
the *Ur-Sprache*,
the babble we once shared

and whether it reappears unwittingly
in a mother's lulling of a child,
the dialects of love,
our gestures when another suffers pain,
the will to give.

These are the bricks
we've always used to build
not only towers and walls
but simple, open places where we can live and breathe   25
and may do still.

The Great Pyramid at Ghiza

We all crave mystery, but more
want mystery dispelled.
And so the goddess on the pedestal
brought down to earth becomes a whore
and we chase dreams
we do not want to wake from.

Schliemann's search, for instance,
the tumulus he dug through
destroying the strata that were Troy,
so that the gold Sophia wore
was made a thousand years
before the siege in Homer's *Iliad*.

And now the pyramids –
the cramped, descending corridors,
chambers we long to penetrate,
leaving no stone unturned,
as if the sun king's spirit
affronted our own mortality.

But whatsoever afterlife he hoped for's
come to this – Fox TV
showing the breakthrough live
as a hushed voiceover fills
the space with trivia.

Is this the pharoah's curse?
That there's no mystery to find?
The sun engorged
by Cairo's dust,
and its neon hieroglyphs?

Rain

I have learned to live with it,
the crystal insects pitting
the windowpane, its cold sting;
no longer turn my face away
when it falls, or I fall in the face
of it.
       Now as I look, cloud
comes over and it begins to rain,
and globules run like tears
down the face of the glass.
But I am walking out into it,
accepted and reclaimed,
its prodigal son.

Aesop

That the life of this most fabled man
is itself a fable, riddled with half-truths,
amuses me, who can't decide whose
story to believe: mine or yours.

You complain: I never opened
myself to you, I never gave.
But who is to decide where we went wrong?
Was Aesop from Thrace or Phrygia;

was he thrown from the cliffs of Delphi
to his death as punishment
for theft or sacrilege; was he a stammerer,
and hideous, or made to seem so by his gift for words?

You were the heights I could not climb.
Stoned by my shortcomings I cannot speak.
I am broken-winded. I am a warning cairn.
I am the moral drawn: Look before you leap!

A Glass Bead Necklace

FOR FRANCINE

There is nothing I do not desire you to have.
I give you this rope of midnight,
I bring you these handfuls of rain,
that our differences sink like stones beneath the sea.

Like a river you flowed through the broken
landscape of my life,
breaking my defenses down.
You carried me to the open sea.

The summer follows you.
At night your body is the hearth
where I am blown back into flame.

I think of all the roads
we travelled before we met, the roads
that spelled our different destinies.

I would be mere darkness were it not for you.

In the desert
we spaded a clear space in the spinifex
and slept under the stars.

We camped among bloodwoods.
We heard of broken promises in the rain.

These glass beads were made in a stone crucible.
They are the Aegean,
they are Freya's eyes,
they are the colour of the sea
the morning Joshua was born –

They will come into our children's hands
and be held as the words for blue are held:
cobalt, indigo, ultramarine, lapis lazuli.

Dubrovnik

For five days under the signal hill
imagining myself sheltering, shelled,
and each night walking stone walls
like Hamlet above the sea,

the Adriatic's heavy swells
like an unmade bed, maternal for all
eternity, as we for whom
no war was waged write postcards home.

On Stradun's marble slabs,
polished by the pedestrian centuries,
Maja speaks of the months
without water, the stench

of sewage, the uncollected trash –
wrongs that right no wrongs,
but weigh on the mind
like unpaid debts or a squandered legacy.

Yet roofs are retiled,
pines no longer bleed,
the rebuilt Conference Centre hosts
our Seminar on Peace,

and sidewalks cratered by cluster bombs
fill with rain. Only the sea
refuses to file away the evidence,
punishing repeatedly this coast
that will not learn its history.

Munch in Stockholm

These rivers, these roads
that are like rugs
pulled from under us,
on which we are
borne into darkness
or, bridged, allow
a moment's reverie or reprieve.

The children especially,
staring or stricken
as the pastel course
swirls and tugs
underfoot
and snow melts,
trees lose their leaves.

The banker who built
this white estate
died in penury;
Sweden redeemed his losses
as this museum.

Hardship is anarchic,
befalling like the bloodshot sky
those walking late,
or the tall ship
rounding the final island of the archipelago.

What goes round, as the saying goes,
comes around,
ghosts of things unrealised
on this stone cold Stockholm day,
and I remember the black pitch cataract
falling through a thousand and one nights . . .

But suddenly there is
a gravel path, a car,
a bridge,
and the foreshore where you are framed
against the light.

Harvard Hire

How can I not think of
those others in their tens of thousands,
spent, sick and in despair,
the degrading lines
from which one was selected to survive
because she could play a cello or violin
while others 'who carried stone'
and were dispensable
escaped only the insult of randomness?

Here on this threshold to
a life some see as unfairly fortunate,
selected because of nothing I have ever done
for gain, the six-figure salary,
and so-called 'privilege',
I conjure the links connecting me to them,
the arbitrary beginnings, the arbitrary ends,
our names made common in the selfsame slot of time,
not even history finding significance
in our extinction or success.

And where that gauntlet of smoke
lunges upward from the dreadful chimney stacks
into a sky as ashen as the earth
and the impassive faces,
I see two cypresses at a quarry's edge
the blue range beyond
outlasting me, neither my doing
nor my witnesses.

Reading William James

I recall the way that we were taught
our syntax – verbs were 'doing words',
adjectives 'described' – and how I lived
not nouns but words like these:
a string of ifs and buts and bys and ands,
determinedly transitive.

Fences go up, and concrete walls
to keep barbarians at bay; shards
of broken glass and razor wire
protect our own. But day after day
bird flight and the tides ceaselessly insist
on subtler shadings for what we feel.

'Reality is where things happen'
writes William James. There is 'a more'
that fringes like a reef the deep self-satisfied
lagoon we think is safe. And surf
breaks distantly at night, bringing the
lesson home that separate names
do not mean separate things.

A Genealogy of Poems

I wrote my first poem about the rain
in longhand at a school desk, lonely.

First one I typed was on a Remington.
It gave me confidence.

And then that portable whose name
I've forgotten, and the midnight poems

of unrequited love
or the longing to get away.

Then there were years of poetry
on the backs of envelopes and bills,

lost lines, fugitive images
looking, like me, for somewhere they belonged

before I bought my Studio 45.
It no longer works, but I keep it just the same

for it shared with me in writing *Latitudes*
and *Wall*, and *Going On*.

I see it now on my rimu writing desk
in Palmerston, the window and the cabbage tree,

the hills I stared at waiting for words to come.
Today the copper roofs of the Danish Parliament,

and three tall chimneys plumed with smoke
are the view I have, and a screen that hums

as I softly sculpt this poem whose genealogy
owes everything

to the ghost in the machine
to pines and sea and seagull's wings

that were the paper, ink and nib I started with,
white shells picked up at Hukuwai

where the sand is ironblack, like the metal
behemoth I first laboured on to speak.

South Coast Journey

BILL MAUGHAN 1940–2002

On a bitter Saturday
I travel east by train,

one of my oldest friends
this morning dead.

I covered his swollen hands with mine
and said goodbye,

this shipwreck of a man, this effigy
he became.

Now like reading a rosary
the coastal towns slip

through my fingers
and I remember him back to life,

the dismembered sculpture
of his first wife in the Judas tree

his jazz LPs, Kid Ory, Beiderbecke,
melting in the fire

as if creative genius were something
one had to sacrifice

to the sphinx of that provincial
town we wound up in.

Yet always his irreverence
shattering our complacencies,

his pure intolerance of shit,
the apocalyptic preacher's eye,

so that I wonder now what I might give
to win that madness back,

and whether it might have sheltered him
from dying young.

But the tide is on the turn, and it is not
whether we will die, but only how,

and who goes first, and when.
Neither does virtue, vice, or meaning

wrung like tears make any difference,
mudflats suffering the cry of birds,

all movements small, like beads
through fingers, and as puppet-like

as on this lurching train
I go away, go east, go on.

House of Masks

I am living in a house of masks
dark-brown, raffia-bearded, slit-eyed or
eyeless, bereft of whatever life they had.

The owner has gone to the Cameroons,
undoubtedly for more, and I must live
with these ominous, fibred masks, drawn

from bush or stream, embodiments
of the wilderness, metaphors for what
we can't control or comprehend.

The owner has pinned up messages for me –
*Please ensure you water the plants. Occasionally
clean the floor and dust all surfaces.*

His inscrutable masks
look down on me as I do his bidding
or sit and watch the evening news on his TV.

What would they attest to
if they could talk? The traces of dried blood,
the black pods, red threads, and broken mirrors?

And when in Sierra Leone the fighting ends,
will dancers put on these masks
for the sake of peace, or will it be to chaos that they return?

Love Poem

By 'proprietary' we mean first that men lay claim to
particular women as songbirds lay claim to territories, as
lions lay claim to a kill, or both sexes lay claim to valuables.
— Margo Wilson and Martin Daly, *The Adapted Mind:
Evolutionary Psychology and the Generation of Culture* (1992)

My eyes lay claim to thee;
you wear a ring to seal the pact that made you mine.
Thus bound, belovèd,
I count thee among my valuables,
a trophy won, the rarest vintage wine.

Be not afraid of my devouring love,
the lion that brands you with his breath;
thou art the range he marks,
the country he now calls his own,
in life and longing and in death.

And if I sing thy praises, like a lark
or swallow hovering above the hill,
know that all I feel for you is in my bones;
I cannot change it; I am likewise tied
to these savannahs where I hunt and kill.

Master-slave relationship, indeed!
Our life, my love, is for the common weal,
our species pressing on to brighter things,
our offspring's future in our genes,
preprogrammed with the feelings that we feel.

40

Please remember that in eternity
in the final 'scheme of things'
we'll have an equal share
in keeping things the way they have to be,
in keeping things the way they were.

Arthur Boyd 1920–1999

I think of a circle of standing stones,
falling one by one as the night comes on,

or is it the falling darkness that makes them
seem to fall, darkness swarming

into the spaces around the dolmen
like wasps smoked out from a hidden hive?

And what is to become of us,
left with your landscapes and fretful

memories of dying unrecognised?
Who will navigate now that the stones are gone?

Who will determine the solstice,
who gather the wild honey and make mead?

I do not know why I so sorely need
you to be alive. I who have no ancestors,

own no stretch of the Shoalhaven,
or cottage in the English countryside,

adrift between Europe, Africa,
and the antipodes, half seer, half blind.

Remembering my Russian

FOR GALINA LINDQUIST

In Russian there is no word for anger,
though the Russian word for love
is one of the most sensuous in the world.

I remember the lessons I took in your language,
the word for river – the river that is
'moving and not moving'

and the word for love. Could once describe
birches against the snow, the frozen Neva
and translate those lines

from Akhmatova's *Requiem*,
the woman approaching her
outside the prison in Leningrad,

lips blue with cold, and asking:
'Can you describe this?'
And she, who had kept vigil

for seventeen months, hoping to see her son,
answering: 'I can.' But with no word
for anger, and not using the word for love.

Now, Galina, you speak of the changes,
as one might speak of dawn and dusk.
But the war goes on in Chechnya.

The homeless die in the frozen snow,
and there is no word for anger
and we have forgotten the word for love.

Trying to Read Heidegger

Distracted from *Sein und Zeit*
by the kids just back from the kiosk,
I make sure they've shared
their bounty equally before
returning to 'the priority
of *existentia* over *essentia*,
and the fact that Dasein is in
each case mine'.

'Open my Kinder Surprise!' my
daughter asks, and then more petulant,
'Dad, can you open it, please . . .'
And so I do, assembling a plastic landscape
with a child and dog
before considering the things
that distract us from
'the pre-phenomenal basis we are seeking':

My children's notion of what is fair.
Two candles lit on the window sill.
My wife due back from shopping in an hour.
Being-in-the-world.
This sense of home.

Living Abroad

We exiles miss its landscapes most.
1° in Copenhagen and I count the cost

of having no hills to walk on
or an ironsand beach, that mystery

of the physical – four elements
rather than ruins or runic stones –

but would not want its emptiness again,
that unflagging sense that one is not oneself

with wilderness, and needs the depths
of history to fathom where one stands

and still may go. Over espressos in
Sebastapol, Ghassan and I recount

journeys to Sierra Leone and Lebanon,
nostalgic no longer for the banalities

of sun and surf and *après-ski*, and I think
back to McCahon's landscape with too few lovers

and Diogenes who, asked where his home was,
answered 'the world'.

Conference

All morning the sere and fallow fields
unreeling, the sun struck from sheet metal,
and the *aark* of crows . . .

Travelling by bus to Fyn
for a conference on 'difference',
being away from work, being out of time.

Though in me is a craving to be alone
on an estuary, rowing down
to the store for provisions on an ebbing tide,

at night steamed cockles with black
bread and Dalmatian wine,
the silence broken only by the chugging

of a boat towing barges of lime
downstream in the darkness,
and the ghost of an old friend

rummaging in the kitchen, stoking
the pot-bellied stove with manuka
and cursing his martyrdom.

In time there is little to be said;
the allotted seasons turn, drab or burgeoning,
without rhyme or reason. The manuka burns,

and stories lose their plot, thumbprints
of scrub or furze, and the scribbled signature
of a fox in freshly fallen snow.

Resurfacing the Road

They are tar-sealing our street this morning,
a black slick, and the smell of it
in my nostrils, men in black
working around witches' hats
and a cone of hot pitch
coating the scraped surface.

But my thoughts are of Eric
at Girton in '71 complaining
that life had passed him by;
playing Leonard Cohen long into the night,
drinking whisky straight
and chain-smoking,
the rough roads shadowing him.

Since he died, the street's
been resurfaced several times,
the same black bitumen
steaming as the workers spread it
around the stormwater drains
and manhole covers.

Viaticum

That all roads led to Rome, we know,
but what of all those bygone travellers,
the provisions and allowances
that saw them on their way – the litter
or the cart, the nuts and dates
and honeyed bread and wine,
coins to grease a palm or pay a toll?

And then the Eucharist for those near death,
as if the afterlife were also on a road
and prayers were grave goods for
their migrant souls.
So many crossroads and cross-purposes.
Imagine the gridlock
after earthquake, fire and flood!

Now it's all humdrum. No laden
hampers or talisman against the evil eye,
no provender 'just in case'. There's
a sign for food and toilets every 20 miles,
a *Burger King*, *McDonald's*, fish and chips,
yet still I carry your photograph
and bear in mind your words
that sent me on my way –

Take care. I love you. Come back soon.
Call us when you can.

New Year's Eve 2004

When the sea withdrew
black rocks appeared
like animals;
then came the overwhelming wave.

Fireworks crackle and explode
over the roofs of Copenhagen;
rock music pounds
in our neighbour's apartment.

Three days ago, Susan Sontag
died, who wrote against
our home-grown terrors
and hypocrisies.

Another year turns,
with still no evidence
of any necessary connection
between the tragic and the good,

And every reason for us to live.

En Famille

Christmas over, my wife and I sit
on the floor of our living room
sorting through family photographs,
slipping them one by one into
the transparent sleeves of an album;
a kind of harvest, perhaps,
on which we'll feed for years,
these last few days arrested forever,
our kids happy, our own lives
apparently in our hands.

Hard to reckon with when
chemicals will seep
from the paper, images stain
and blur, and we become
strangers to our own descendants,
who'll have to guess at what we did
and who we were.

Why give memory anything
to get its hands on,
why bequeath our lives to be interpreted
by others when they will have theirs?
Better to enter the coming year
with empty hands,
nothing to lose,
nothing we can share.

Dead Reckoning

There's a gold weather-vane –
a galleon – catching the sun
on the sea-green copper
spire of Sankt Johannes,
not a cloud in the sky,
the ship as if becalmed.

I try to recall
the currents, compass
errors and storms that took me
off course, asking
whether, and for how long
one's initial bearing lasts.

But on a windless day like this
the fifteen-metre waves
the broken mast
the ice-jammed pulley-block
are long forgotten
and it seems one is

exactly where one planned
to be, having kept
for all these years
with sextant and calipers
dead reckoning,
and come home.